Naming the Trees

Ness Owen

Arachne Press

First published in UK 2025 by Arachne Press Limited
100 Grierson Road, London, SE23 1NX
www.arachnepress.com
© Ness Owen 2025

ISBNs
Print: 978-1-913665-95-1 eBook: 978-1-913665-96-8

The moral rights of the author have been asserted. All rights reserved. This book is sold subject to the condition that it shall not, by way of trade or otherwise, be lent, resold, hired out or otherwise circulated without the publisher's prior written consent in any form or binding or cover other than that in which it is published and without similar condition including this condition being imposed on the subsequent purchaser. Except for short passages for review purposes no part of this publication may be reproduced, stored in a retrieval system or transmitted in any form or by any means, electronic, mechanical, photocopying, recording or otherwise, without prior written permission of Arachne Press.

Cover design © Lou Moore

Thanks to Muireann Grealy and Sian Northey for their proofreading.

Arachne Press acknowledges the financial support of the Books Council of Wales.

EU GPSR contact for product safety information
outreach@arachnepress.com, Gorica 17, Radovljica, Gorenjska, 4240, Slovenija
see also our website arachnepress.com/GPSR

Printed in the UK.

Acknowledgements

I wish to thank the editors of the following publications where versions of some of the poems first appeared: Dreich, Red Poets, Black Bough Journal, Cinnamon Press, Seventh Quarry.

I am grateful to the BBC for permission to publish the *Penrhos* sequence of poems which were commissioned for the BBC Radio 4 programme *United Kingdoms* and broadcast on January 31st, 2022. Special thanks to the producer Emma Harding.

To Lou Moore for the inspiring *The Battle for the Trees* exhibition from which the cover image is taken.

Many thanks to Cherry, Saira and to all my poetry friends for supporting my work and their kind words and encouragement. Much gratitude to Cath Drake and her inspiring Veranda project where some of the poems began.

Huge thanks to the #LadiesofPenrhos and forces of nature: Hilary, Lisa, Sharon, Bernie and all in the Achub Penrhos/ Save Penrhos team campaigning to keep Penrhos as a community nature reserve.

And Then the Geese Turned Up was the winning poem in Greenpeace UK's Poem for the Planet 2022.

Ffraid and *Gwenfaen* were written for and exhibited in Unus Multorum Project (2020) as *Daeth y mor a nhw – The sea brought them* collaboration with artist Rita Jones. Much thanks to Julie Upmeyer.

To Dad who showed me how raindrops silvered the trees.
Diolch a chariad mawr bob amser i'r tri G a C.
Diolch o galon.

NOTES

Jill Lepore quotation taken from *What We Owe Our Trees* (newyorker.com, 2023)

It is through my body that the world acts on me – quotes taken from *A philosopher on the true meaning of 'my body, my choice'* by Fiona Woolard (theconversation.com, 2022)

Much of the Welsh tree-lore in the poems derives from *Folk-lore and Folk-stories of Wales* by Marie Trevelyan (1909), the rest is remembered from stories I was told as a child.

Tishani Doshi quotation from *In Praise of Shape Poetry*, an article on Poetry Foundation website.

Anne Carson quotation from *The Glass Essay* in *Glass Irony and God* (New Directions Publishing Corporation, 1995)

Robin Wall Kimmerer quotation from *Gathering Moss: A Natural and Cultural History of Mosses* (Oregon State University Press, 2003)

The quoted translation from *The Book of Taliesin VIII* is from *The Four Ancient Books of Wales*, W. F. Skene, 1858

The quotation heading *Hawthorn is for the Heart-strong* is my own (mis)translation from the old Welsh:
Pan swynhwyt godeu.
Y gobeith an godeu.

Trees are Our Life uses, and responds to, phrases found in government documents about the Forest for Wales.

Naming the Trees

Rubbing the moon dust from our eyes,
we keep walking
(and some days this is more than enough)

Contents

Introduction	8
Penrhos Sequence	10
1. Show Us What it is to Love a Forest With Song	12
2. How Easy is it to Lose Ourselves?	14
3. Where Estuary Meets Sea	16
4. Walk With Us	18

I

Naming the Trees	20
Ash is for the Dreamers	21
Sky Looked Down and Tried not to Judge	22
In Winter's Path	24
Llwybr y Gaeaf	25
Gathering for Calennig	26
Hel ar gyfer Calennig	27
Waiting for Rhiannon's Birds	28
Cerddinnen *Rowan to Guard Us*	29
And Then the Geese Turned Up	30
Yna cyrhaeddodd y gwyddau	32
A Riot of Bluebells on Their Own Would Only be a Tantrum	34
Daffodils are Dangerous	36
Birch is for Love	37
Llygad Ebrill	38
Ode to Ragwort	40
Sycamore's Choice	42
Trees are Our Life	44
Coed yw Ein Bywyd	46

Elder Bleeds When Cut	48
II	
Hazel for Wishing	50
Adra	51
Mudprints in Cae Morfa	52
Hawthorn is for the Heart-strong	53
Butterfly Count in Gorsedd y Penrhyn Meadow	54
The Hunt	56
Beech for Our Protection	57
Waking the Sea Saints: Ffraid	58
Gwenfaen	59
Heuldro'r Haf (The Sun-turn of Summer)	60
It is Through my Body that the World Acts on Me	61
Agor y Clawdd	62
What the Thunder Really Wanted to Say	63
Note to Self	64
Elm to Stand and Fight	65
Hushed	66
Hold Each Word	67
And One Day You'll be Wearing the Wrong T-Shirt	68
Oak to Breathe Old Secrets	70
One Foot in Front of Another	71
Walking Home	72

Introduction

We are often asked, as writers, why we write, and there are of course many different reasons. For me, being very much a writer of place, it usually starts from my *cynefin*: to bear witness, to share, to send a story out into the world.

This collection was inspired by Penrhos which is a much treasured nature reserve and forest on Beddmanarch Bay, an Area of Outstanding National Beauty and SSSI, on Ynys Cybi. It is the only accessible woodland on the small island. Originally part of the Stanley family estate, it was thought to be gifted to the local community in 1971 by Anglesey Aluminium.

It is a haven for wildlife including endangered red squirrels, ancient woodland, bats, fungi and thousands of migrating birds. It has been a nature reserve for the whole of my life and as for many others, it was very much part of my childhood. There are garlands of Penrhos stories to tell. Penrhos is part of our community history, heritage and wellbeing.

In 2016, planning permission was granted for a holiday complex that would mean the felling of many trees and the end to the majority of public access.

The Achub Penrhos/Save Penrhos campaign is led by a small group of women who have gained followers and supporters from Ynys Môn and all over the world. Together with the many Penrhos supporters, they have campaigned, protested and fundraised thousands to legally appeal against this decision.

What else would I tell you about Penrhos other than, if you can, go there yourselves. Walk the paths, walk the seasons, or virtually visit:

Facebook: Save Penrhos Coastal Park
Twitter: @PenrhosSave
Instagram: @savepenrhos_achubpenrhos

The fight continues to protect and preserve this beloved place for our future generations, just as other campaigns continue to fight to save their green spaces.

As Richard Llwyd (1752-1835) wrote in his poem 'Lines Addressed to the Thrush, in the garden at Penrhos'

And now, proud leader of the feather'd throats,
Long may fair Penrhos with thy voice be blest

Penrhos

Mae'r onnen ar gyfer y breuddwydwyr
Ash is for the dreamers

Y gerddinen yw ein gwarcheidwad
Rowan to guard us

Mae'r fedwen ar gyfer cariad
Birch for love

Mae'r ysgawen yn gwaedu pan gaiff ei thorri
Elder to bleed when cut

Mae'r gollen ar gyfer dymuniadau
Hazel for wishing

Mae'r ddraenen wen ar gyfer y galon-gryf
Hawthorn for the heart-strong

Mae'r ffawydd yn ein hamddiffyn
Beech for our protection

Mae'r llwyfen yn sefyll ei thir
Elm to stand and fight

Mae'r Dderwen yn anadlu hen gyfrinachau
Oak to breathe old secrets

1. Show Us What it is to Love a Forest with Song

In this our imagined future
we watch them sound the trees
hoping for deadwood, knowing

the living are always harder to cut.
Ivy holds fast as roots are cleared,
heartbeats counted from face-cut

to fall in chorus of chainsaw-snarl,
creak and thud, till a parcel of birds
wakes us, carrying us back to their

rowdy shore. Oystercatchers, wading
the wrinkle of tide, announce our
arrival, call us back to our cynefin[1]

(a place where we belong)

to seagrass sweet air, layers of path
awaiting. Sycamore reaches out her
arms, invites our first forest breath,

unravelling muscle memories of before
we learnt to run. We are leaving the
Alpoco factory-hum behind, chimney

shadow, distant Cob-Road thump,
turning ourselves to leaf whisper,
lull of branch murmur. Footfall echoes,

as we tread into the hush of our steps,
let the curve of the track embrace us,
wait for that first forest bird to take

up tune, to show us what it is to
love a forest with song. Under
willow arch, velvet-moss bound.

[1] A difficult to translate word literally meaning habitat, but with a deeper meaning of a place where someone belongs (Welsh)

2. How Easy is it to Lose Ourselves?

To stray on fox path,
trail red squirrel chase
among branches, step

through the ivy-choked
to forgotten gardens and
find ourselves in the ruins?

We come here to undo the day,
ymhyfrydu, llonyddu, tawelu²

to follow our noses/feed our souls,
ease our minds/walk with our
departed/to connect/revive/
find leaf magic/breathe salt-wind,
hold our ground/
trust the path to be kind.

And in these moments

we are holly-green,
lichen splashed,
roots exposed,

heads tipped to ground
craving the kinship
beneath our feet, knitting

the forest together, for
tree-tongue to teach us
the language of giving

as mother trees give
their all and we might
unlearn our dislocation.

[2] delight in, calm, quieten

3. Where Estuary Meets Sea

We spy with Tunnicliffe
eyes, sketching our winters

in shimmering flocks of
plover, curlew, brent geese
revelling in their mudflat

bounty while egrets fly
against the tides and
rain begins its fall.

We dream of dog-dragged
summer scrambles to
Gorsedd y Penrhyn –

and Arthur's Seat through
painted-lady meadow
dandelion blazed, in

oxeye daisy finale
and grasshopper rattle.
Or in the stillness of the

dew-webbed, season of
spiders where we watch
the faraway world turn,

clouds gather and scatter
over Mynydd y Garn.
They tell us good fortune

will come to those,
who walk barefoot on
Beddmanarch sands

then turn away to king
-fisher wish past the
ripple of Scouts pond.

Falling deeper into
derw, llwyfen, onnen,
cerddinen, bedwen,
ffawydden, ysgawen[3]

[3] oak, elm, ash, rowen, birch, beech, elder

4. Walk With Us

Watch season stand

                                      Ash is for the dreamers

and surrender to season.

                                      Rowan to guard us

See how even on

                                        Birch for love

the darkness days,

                                      Elder to bleed when cut

in the canopy shade,

                                        Hazel for wishing

light rays strike

                                  Hawthorn for the heart-strong

through the crown shyness

                                    Beech for our protection

and for some days this

                                    Elm to stand and fight

is more than enough.

                                 Oak to breathe old secrets.

I
With the forest go the worlds within those woods
Jill Lepore

Naming the Trees
finding the words is another step in learning to see
Robin Wall Kimmerer

The more I sit with you
the less I'm sure
your leaves tell one story
your bough another.

You speak in layers,
leaf litter,
mor, moder, mull.

How would we capture you
in just one word?

We name you the sound of the wind
in your leaves
We name you the animal that
you draw near.

We name you bud, flower, fruit
We name you to keep you alive
We name you to keep you with us.

Ash is for the Dreamers
Fe ddaw Gŵyl Fair, fe ddaw Gŵyl Ddewi,
fe ddaw'r adar bach i ganu

And if you ever find
yourself here,
before the promise of
spring, not knowing
what direction to take,
turn by the castled tower
past the familiar creak
of pine, into the path of
ash trees and rest
under their airy grace
where light reaches
for the floor.

It's all too easy to forget
the gentle awe of buds
curving to sun.
Don't you just owe it
to yourself to become
a dreamer again?
Take off your gloves,
draw diamonds in bark.
Trust your detours
and redirections.
Pick up a leaf,
wear it close.

Sky Looked Down and Tried not to Judge

Panoramic vision is not always
a blessing. There's a time when the low cloud
must lift. What has been seen can't be forgotten.

Ground had always been so open
disclosing disturbances lost and abandoned
there should be no secrets between them.

Looking for goodness takes practice
she knew. Didn't pointing your fingers
mean fingers will be pointed back?

How easy would it be to
lose herself in vastness of desert,
escape into the enormity of seas?

Experience told her disengage, limit
exposure, looking away she turned to her
colour palette to see what she could muster:

nothing but bleached bone, arid alabaster.
Her gaze drew back, meeting the jammed
arteries of a morning rush hour,

rodded skeletons of abandoned factories,
oily boat trails bequeathed to sea depths.
Thoughts flickered in her thermosphere.

What would she do? What could she change?
Could she be hero or villain?
How would she take action?

Skirting cliff edges for answers
resting in mountain-heather's quiet
embrace, she focused on gorse in her

loudest yellow, finding pockets of hope
in a parcel of trees, persistence in a
thoughtful chough digging for worm.

And she returned to what she did best
scattering her blueness, hoping to stir
the small town bleeding outwards.

In Winter's Path

We expect to see no one

all doors are safely shut at

Mari Lwyd[4] time when we

know, we can be defeated

by a song.

The trees bared

show their true shape, soft

dead-wood holds life beneath

our feet. There's little to hide

behind, on walks like these.

---

[4] Grey Mare – a Welsh tradition where a horse-figure is carried from door to door by singing groups during the Christmas season.

Llwybr y Gaeaf.

Disgwyliwn weld neb *â'r*

holl ddrysau ar gau yn ddiogel

yn amser y Fari Lwyd pan

fyddwn yn gwybod, gallwn

gael ein trechu gan gân.

Heb ddail, mae coed yn dangos

eu gwir ffurfiau, coed crin sy'n dal

bywyd dan ein traed. Nid oes

llawer i'w guddio y tu ôl, ar

deithiau fel y rhain.

Gathering for Calennig[5]

Raindrops pearl the hawthorns

as dusk powders a promising sky

our holly's berries are already lost

so we must gather our sticks wisely.

White and blackthorn never agree,

elder would weep and willow is

for the broken-hearted. Soft

sycamore is carved for love so

we choose her broken branches.

---

[5] An old Welsh New Year's tradition where an apple is decorated with evergreens and skewered on three sticks for collecting gifts and luck.

Hel ar gyfer Calennig

Mae diferion glaw yn perlio'r ddraenen wen

fel y cyfnos yn lliwio awyr addawol

mae aeron ein celyn eisoes ar goll

felly rhaid i ni ddewis ein ffyn yn feddylgar.

Nid yw'r ddraenen wen a'r ddraenen ddu byth yn cytuno,

byddai ysgawen yn wylo a'r helyg

yn cysuro y drylliedig. Mae'r sycamorwydden

feddal yn cael ei cherfio am gariad felly

dewiswn ei changhennau toredig.

Waiting for Rhiannon's Birds

We willed that one

      day we'd hear their

bewildering song carried

      along the curve of our

           shore, lulling us from

      these waking dreams,

as seaweed prayer flags

      flutter on barbed-wire

           fences and the sky leans

                to hush the earth.

      Who would we choose

           to rouse?

Cerddinen[6]
Rowan to Guard Us

All winter
I thought
that I'd lost you.
The toughest of
survivors they said
so I tended your
bareness, willed for
the poem in you to
bud, watched for
pinnacle fingers,
waited for the
berries I would
sew in hemlines
to guard all that
I have ever loved.

[6] Rowan

Then the Geese Turned Up

It wasn't until the brent geese arrived, dark
bellies ravenous for eelgrass, that we really
started to worry with their constant ronking
and cronking they weren't about to give up
their winter bounty. Someone said they fly
at night, use the moon and stars like they
owned them, never left anyone behind
like a skein of true soldiers but worse still
these poets always want to write about them.

Our reasoning fell on covered ears:
Why would you deny us a high quality
destination leisure village, five hundred chalets,
luxury spa and water sports centre?
So, we lose a few old trees. We will of
course replant them. Jet skiers have rights
too and any way you tootle off each
summer. A wheel of lapwings heckled
past *some of us, you know, are here to stay.*

Little red breast had been so easy
to coax, eating out of our hands, posing
for a photo or two, all for mealworm
promise. We reminded woodpecker of
damage already done and a bit about
glass houses. We resisted the rowdy
oystercatchers' taunts *leave us be, build
somewhere else.* So easy to ignore distant
red glares from unlicenced cockle-beds.

But these geese they wouldn't let it go.

Uniting with haunting curlew and solitary
sandpipers. Their honeyed songs graced
the air as one and all the calls we'd heard
before were harsh compared to them and
all this time the mudflats sang, the tide
swept in, sea lavender bloomed and withered,
sea pink carpeted her mid-marsh ground,
ragworms carried on their business regardless.

Yna Cyrhaeddodd y Gwyddau

Nid tan i'r gwyddau du gyrraedd, a'u boliau
tywyll yn newynu am wellt y gamlas,
y dechreuon ni boeni o ddifrif gyda'u honcian
a'u croncian nad oeddent ar fin rhoi'r gorau
i'w gwledd aeaf i neb. Dywedodd rhywun eu bod
yn hedfan yn y nos, yn defnyddio'r lleuad a'r sêr
fel pe taent yn berchen arnynt, byth yn gadael neb ar ôl
fel edafedd o filwyr go iawn ond yn waeth byth mae
beirdd bob amser eisiau ysgrifennu amdanyn nhw.

Roedd ceisio rhesymu â nhw yn anobeithiol:
Pam fyddech chi'n gwadu i ni, bentref hamdden
o ansawdd uchel, pum cant o gabanau, sba moethus
a chanolfan chwaraeon dŵr? Felly beth os ydym
yn colli ychydig o hen goed. Byddwn wrth gwrs yn eu
hailblannu. Mae gan sgiwyr jet hawliau
hefyd a beth bynnag rydych chi'n gadael pob
haf. Roedd olwyn o gornchwiglod yn heclo wrth
iddynt fynd heibio: *Mae rhai ohonom yma i aros.*

Roedd y robin bach lleol wedi bod mor hawdd i'w
berswadio, yn bwyta allan o'n dwylo, yn sefyll
am lun neu ddau, i gyd am yr addewid o fwydod.
Fe wnaethom atgoffa cnocell y coed am ddifrod
oedd eisoes wedi'i wneud ac am aderyn glân yn canu.
Troesom ein cefn ar wawd y bioden fôr.
Gadewch lonydd i ni, adeiladwch rywle arall.
Mae mor hawdd anwybyddu llacharedd coch
yn y pellter o welyau cocos didrwydded.

Ond fyddai'r gwyddau ddim yn rhoi'r gorau iddi.

Unwyd y gylfinir a phibyddion unig. Roedd eu
caneuon mêl yn swyno'r awyr fel un
a'r holl alwadau a glywsom o'r blaen yn llym
o'u cymharu â nhw. Parhaodd y gwastadeddau
llaid i ganu, y llanw'n ysgubo i mewn,
y lafant y môr yn blodeuo ac yn gwywo,
y clustog fair yn carpedu ar dir canol y gors,
y mwydod yn cario ymlaen â'u busnes, dibryder.

A Riot of Bluebells on Their Own
Would Only be a Tantrum

We all knew the bluebells
had been known to combine
and cause commotion, arriving
as they always do, a gush of blue,
sweeping across the undergrowth,
shaking their flame-like stamens
when we're already primrose
struck – the perfect distraction.

But they weren't alone,
wild garlic was never far
behind, a real crowd pleaser.
People came from miles away
and left scented with their aroma.

Guelder rose and hard fern
were suspected too but
perhaps a little too obvious
as strong reminders of
half-remembered forests
and far too old and clever,
most probably quiet inciters.

So how do we proceed,
get further in with lichen
in every corner listening?

Of course the powerful
always lie underground
below the understory and
not one of them will give
them away only their old
Woodland-was-here
Woodland-was-here story.

They seem to have settled
into winter but without their
canopy how long can they
last? And I suspect they'll
be quiet again now they
know we're watching.
Don't you agree?

Daffodils are Dangerous

The daffodils were ablaze ready that March/we picked the ones that commanded our attention/wore them daringly through the day/like the warriors we wished to be/it was sunny/we were alive in green and yellow/after school/after supper/we hid in the side-garden/where no one could see us/ate a daffodil between us/six petals separated into loves and loves me not/sugar-coated so we could swallow/but it wasn't until after/did we learn of their poison/not the fatal kind/but still enough for our heads to dip/our backs to arch with the weight of knowing/pretty could be poisonous/we could be our own ruin/so we laid down in the sea of dead-grass/three ladies of Shallot/and promised to never speak of flowers/we were good at keeping secrets/good at being quiet/and we waited for it to take us away from this one life/ but this time it didn't/we were still the same but somehow different/we were sepal, petal, pollen dust/mass and joy of many/we stood up/left the garden/walked away from the dead-grass/golden hearts tilted ready/our skin would replace itself/our bones would grow old and tell our story/we daffodils are dangerous/we bear our boldness softly.

Birch is for Love
Why hold onto all onto all that? And I said
Where can I put it down?
Anne Carson

Aren't you just
the easiest to know?
Always the last to dress.
Paper bark so willing to peel
A bandage ready for wounds.
Bending your softened twigs
we weave a wreath
nestling in your leaves.
There is no way out.

Llygad Ebrill
(April Eyes)[7]

And they
blinked
open
eager hearts
reaching
for a
watery
sun.

True
worshippers
before
leaf
canopy
denies
the grace of
an open sky.

Yellow
facing
blue.
Blue
facing
yellow.

The air is
still sharp.
Bitter winds
from the feet
of the dead
keep us moving,
clinging to their
quiet promise

Joy is to come.

[7]Lesser celandine

Ode to Ragwort

All those years
how we hated you.
The way you'd just appeared,
unannounced.

A blatant splash of
gold, laying claim
to bareness. Places
we'd disown.

We'd gather after rains
to rip you from the earth,
salt your roots, feared
your poison on our skin,
the wind that carried
your seed.

But you always
came back,
determined for more.

This time a nectar god
swarming with life,
swathed in caterpillar
garlands.

A brazen bee-feast
giggling in an autumn-gust
long after summer left.

We wait forever
to count your
petal-fall:
the bad,
the good
the something in between.

Sycamore's Choice

And why would we remember
the curve into darkness
of an overtrodden path,

autumn-swamped

the ease of circling
to not know
the way out,

ache of jaw-clench
as you mutter past
the plastic chime of
a shit bag hung on
lower branch

then from sycamore,

a delicious leap,
a spin, a glide
soft unmasking of
colour holds you
in a warm mosaic,

your arms unfasten
your mind a whorl
of beautiful abandon.

We blamed these sea-winds
for all this shredding
but it always was
a choice, a learning to breathe
with separation.

Trees are Our Life
After Craig Santos Perez

Welcome to the Forest of Cymru
Because our earth has lost a third of its forest
for there are worlds within those woods
as mother trees give up their secrets
seeing they perished once but then returned
given they can be one percent alive and still survive
considering that we came down from the trees
since forest wandering gave us intuition
while tall trees won our wars.

Because our government has a long-term forestation programme
for they want a network of woodland
as they want it the length and breadth of us
seeing as they want to protect nature
given that they want it to be a community venture
considering that they want it accessible to everyone
since they want to support our wellbeing
while they want to plant an idea.

Because they want us to be part of it
for they want to restore and maintain
the irreplaceable, the matchless, the existing,
the current, the present, the living, the being
as we plead with them not to fell our ancient forests
seeing that we ask them not to build a fence to keep us out
given that, in our language, we can dod yn ôl at ein coed[8]
considering that our trees rose in battle
since our trees can half burn
while trees are our lungs, our hearts, our medicine

because forests are our home
because we will return to our trees
because we will keep fighting for our forest
because forests save lives
because forests save lives.

[8]come back to our trees

Coed yw Ein Bywyd
Ar ôl Craig Santos Perez

Croeso i Goedwig Cymru
Oherwydd bod ein daear wedi colli traean o'i choedwig
canys y mae bydoedd o fewn y coedydd hynny
wrth i'r mam goed ddatgelu eu cyfrinachau
achos eu bod wedi marw unwaith ond yna dychwelyd
o ystyried y gallant fod un y cant yn fyw ac yn dal i oroesi
gan ystyried ein bod wedi dod i lawr o'r coed
gan mai crwydro coedwigoedd roddodd reddf i ni
tra enillodd coed uchel ein rhyfeloedd.

Oherwydd bod gan ein llywodraeth raglen goedwigo hirdymor
oherwydd mae arnynt eisiau rhwydwaith o goetir
fel y maent ei eisiau ar ein hyd a'n lled
oherwydd eu bod am amddiffyn natur
o ystyried eu bod am iddi fod yn fenter gymunedol
gan ystyried eu bod am iddi fod yn hygyrch i bawb
gan eu bod am gefnogi ein lles
tra maen nhw eisiau plannu syniad.

Achos maen nhw eisiau i ni fod yn rhan ohoni
canys y maent am adfer a chynnal
yr unigryw, y digyffelyb, y presennol,
y cyfoesol, yr awron, y byw, y bod
wrth inni ymbil arnynt i beidio â thorri ein coedwigoedd hynafol
wrth i ni ofyn iddyn nhw beidio ag adeiladu ffens i'n cadw ni allan
o ystyried y gallwn, yn ein hiaith, ddod yn ôl at ein coed
gan ystyried bod ein coed wedi codi mewn brwydr
oherwydd gall ein coed hanner llosgi
tra mai coed yw ein hysgyfaint, ein calonau, ein meddyginiaeth.

Gan mai coedwigoedd yw ein cartref.
Oherwydd byddwn yn dychwelyd at ein coed.
Oherwydd byddwn yn parhau i ymladd dros ein coedwig.
Oherwydd bod coedwigoedd yn achub bywydau.
Oherwydd bod coedwigoedd yn achub bywydau.

Elder Bleeds When Cut

What rook could ever keep a secret?
Mob hungry for new clecs[9]
sky clattered with pried story
they robe me in their satin shadow
and I am flock thankful
feather befriended.

There is only our song
brush of air, smack of wings
praise of being many,
a language of waiting
darkness calls us home.

Here-here-here,
too-close-too-close

shuffle of claw, recognised kin.
They tell me there is a lesson
in every loss.

Nothing is still.
Elder raises her branches
anticipating berries.
The season will turn.

Know-your-place
know-your-place
know-your-place

[9] Gossip

II

I have been in a multitude of shapes
The Battle of the Trees
The Book of Taliesin VIII

Hazel for Wishing

It was winter when
we found you
looking downwards
as they told us
hazelnuts never fall far.

We shaped a cap,
like they told us,
of twigs and fallen leaves
on the morning
of a new moon.

We placed it on the
bravest of us and
kept watch but
what do you ask for
when you're asking
for everyone and you
know of the woman
that wished herself
away only for someone
else to wish her back?

We balanced it on
the oldest stem.
Wish we said.
Wish for us.

Adra[10]

Perhaps you were born
lime-washed as the houses

on a winter's storm beach
where two seas almost meet

with a people who yield to a
tide that takes no holding as

summer turns Porth to Bay
Rhyd to Ford but we never

will bury our dead.

[10]Home

Mudprints in Cae Morfa[11]

We pressed our wellies
deep into the singing mud
moving in all directions
scarring the Morfa's soft
belly, our last tylwyth-like
dance as sunset gowned
the rocks making gold
of our lichen.

We were pennywort
rich, rock-rose jewelled.
Learning our way from
our mudflat mother
imagining for this once
the tide would not wash
us away and time loved
us enough to keep us
for more than mottled
memories but for these
moments of wonder
to one day be
rediscovered.

[11] Sea-marsh field

Hawthorn is for the Heart-strong
When you enchant trees – hope rises

How can you deny this pull,
this comfort in the twist of boughs?

Lone white-thorn bows to
the sea-wind, seizes sunset

in her branches, holds
warriors beneath her roots,

speaks a language you
must be ready to hear.

Believe she says
believe that things
will get better.

Keep your softness
whisper your troubles
watch how the
sky burns.

Butterfly Count in Gorsedd y Penrhyn Meadow

So we wait, sun casting
rays over our shoulders,
conscious of our shadows,
bone-quiet as instructed
paper list in hands.
Hunched closer to
summer-crisped meadow,
we wish ourselves smaller

hope for the slumber
of the nectar drunk.
Finding comfort in the
slightest flicker,
a chase of gatekeepers,
bursts of amber,
bay and rust.

A sudden synchrony
of small whites
plaiting air with
invisible thread.
We burn to break
our promise of

stillness,
lured into the
beautiful frenzy
of their flight till
Chaffinch chants

her rain-song
to remind us
is it too late –
is it too late?

We hold on to our
shadows, hide what
awful shades we

must throw in their
world of colour,

glorious spectrums of light.

The Hunt

Snow betrays
the tread of your
path,

straight as
the rooks fly
and heckle at
our intrusion.

We follow your
hunt not seeking
blood but to quieten

our heedless thirst
to capture a
small measure
of your world

new
gospels
in your eyes.

Beech for Our Protection

This remembering
of warmth awakened
in February's shadows
in the starkness of
empty branches
standing open
sculpted to the sky.
And it was decided
this year would
be the year of plenty.
The forest needed to feast
and everything was language
a knowingness between them.
Bud burst after bud burst
catkin, flower,
wind shake open
dappled shade
to beech nut flooring.
The forest must eat.
The air is changing.
Our only role
to watch and listen.

Waking the Sea Saints

Ffraid[12]

We know little
other than the sea
brought you when
our time-worn edges
ached to be reminded
that kindness is a choice,
our strength, a force
that lingers. A gift
in a hesitant world.

        Ffraid

        Ychydig a wyddom
        oni bai i'r môr
        dy ddanfon atom pan fo'n
        hymylon lluddedig
        yn erfyn am gael eu hatgoffa
        fod caredigrwydd
        yn ddewis,yn gryfder,
        yn rym sy'n aros.
        Anrheg mewn byd
        petrusgar.

---

[12] A saint said to have travelled on a piece of turf over the Irish Sea and arrived at Trearddur on Ynys Cybi.

Gwenfaen[13]

What are we without
water and the sea-wind
that lets the gull soar?
Like pebbles we fracture
for the sea to etch and
smooth, while angels
watch in white-quartz
stone, the tide will
uncover your joy.

        Gwenfaen

        Beth ydym ni heb
        ddŵr a gwynt y môr
        sy'n gadael i'r wylan esgyn?
        Fel cerrig mân rydym
        yn torri, i'r môr ein hysgythru
        a'n llyfnu. Tra bydd angylion
        yn gwylio mewn cerrig
        gwynion, bydd y llanw'n
        datgelu dy lawenydd.

[13] A saint brought to Ynys Môn by the sea, who was said to be able to soothe minds.

Heuldro'r Hâf
(The Sun-turn of Summer)
At Bryn Celli Ddu[14]

Only

a moment of

solstice light

a transitory break

in the clouds was

enough to lift darkness,

ignite the chamber,

a gift from

the

waning

sun.

---

[14] A Neolithic tomb on Ynys Môn that is aligned to the summer solstice

It is Through my Body that the World Acts on Me

When I wake to
cinnamon sunrise
close my eyes to
gorse-creak
whistle of feather
flush of wild rose
how my body speaks to me
unwrapping ripples of joy
across my skin.

*It is through my body
that I act on the world.*
I use it to pen these words
to unlock these thoughts.
When it's wounded,
I am wounded.

I am
its only keeper.

I know fear,
a racing heartbeat,
hustled breath.
I know anger,
a slammed door,
clenched fist.

I must – I will
have my say.
*my body
my right
my life.*

Agor y Clawdd[15]

As they stabbed and
punctured the years of
entanglement, bramble
invaders reached out

their arms, the gorse
wept her yellow tears
knowing her seeds were
sleeping safely underground.

The wind-bent hawthorn,
*who never did care where
she was placed,* released
a trembling of birds as

her roots were ripped
from the ground.
Earth-scent trickled
from them, warning

others in a language,
too slow to save them,
but maybe one day
we'd understand.

[15] Clearing the Hedgerow

What the Thunder Really Wanted to Say

When they don't listen
               let your voice be
                             a shock wave
                                        splitting air

be afraid of quietness
               stand in front of mirrors
                             pause in open fields

                        NOTICE THE STORM

     tree-shelter
             arrive after a ribbon of light
                       let them count down
                                 to your visits

shout
                    shout
                                   shout

Note to Self

Rip up your lawn
plant a garden,
buy an apple

with a blemish
and park your car.
Stop wasting time

pointing your finger
stop buying things
fashioned to break.

Understand, this time
next year will be worse.
Teach these lessons.

Teach our children.
Learn what we forgot.
Be the truth-teller

waking early, catching
the first bird to take
up their song. Listen.

Mother Earth is always
speaking. If you're waiting
for a sign, this is it.

Elm to Stand and Fight

Begin with a branch,
everything you need
to know is here.
Trace bark stretched
upwards in growth,
leaves sharp as pins,
clefts holding life.
Consider where you
are, slow down and
listen by her side.

(Consider the request)

(State your position)

(Stand your ground)

Some trees don't
follow the rules.
Beware of falling
boughs.

Hushed
Protest is a key tactic for humanity to win

How are our voices to be heard?
Who will listen to the overlooked
the ignored? By banding together
our freedoms have been born.
So who are we now?
Descendants of Beca taking
down the gates, grandchildren
of the Women's Peace Petition
collecting their seven miles of
names, children of Cymdeithas
dumping the uniaith signs?
Peace women marching
a hundred and twenty miles?
Why would we let them
crush our power to stand up
when peaceful protest is a
human right. We must
never forget – Visibility is
revolutionary. Time to let
go of passivity. This liberty
is ours.

Hold Each Word

Language is never just about what is being said;
it is also about how it is held.
Tishani Doshi

Hold each word a little longer
  till echoes fill your ears
and you remember the
  lilt of your tongue

  let the orchestra of
notes find shape in
  your mouth as you
release them to the air

accept no silence
  open the box
open the gates

Fuse your letters
  flaunt your beautiful
        ll, and ch

  borrow, trip, stumble,
        taste life twice
  step out of your apologies

free your apron tongue
  mwydro, janglo, malu awyr[16]
find the rhythm that you forgot

return to what is yours.

[16] moider, jangle, break the air (ways of speaking)

And One Day You'll be Wearing the Wrong T-Shirt

And who knows what that
T-shirt will say as there'll
always be something that
needs saving from us.

Will it be for our-bodies-
languages-or-forests, our-
rivers-mountains-and-seas?
The list stretches further

than our ordinary eyes
perceive. And with all
good intentions you'll
wear it like a shield.

Silvering like a holly blue
knowing that days are short.
Bold as cherry blossom
show stopping the birds.

You'll be chattering like
the sparrows to anyone
that'll listen, summer
giddy as a dunnock for

what you know is right.
You're an optimist if
nothing else and you've
faith that it's not too late.

And maybe you knew this
moment was coming as
you'll stand with your
people smiling at the

skies and they'll tell
you, you're wearing
the wrong T-shirt and
show you how low

is the bar. But who
knows. Just maybe.
You'd wear it again.

Oak to Breathe Old Secrets

And you hold tight to those
secrets in the quiet thrill of
knowing, savouring as summer
spills from your branches and
the sky holds every sort
of cloud, trusting your purpose
of one day revealing, woman
of blossoms, fires brought
from the sun, the wisdom
of an unexceptional life.

One Foot in Front of Another

Things often have a way of falling apart
        before you finally agree to
put one foot in front of another
        firing at least a hundred neurons
you engage every muscle every bone
        (if you think too much it becomes difficult)
gravity is always helpful
        your legs will swing like
pendulums but you must
        always have one foot
in touch with the earth.
        (if you think too much this really becomes difficult)
A cocktail of chemicals shoots
        messages to your brain
(this is not as painful as you imagine)
        find a forest and
breathe in evergreen alleviations.
        If you wanted to add up the bones,
muscles, tendons, ligaments in your feet,
        it would come to a hundred and fifty-nine
all to help you walk away,
        walk back
or to walk towards an answer.

Walking

Home

Tilting our heads

to the stars,

wishing we had names for each

constellation on a night where everything

seems clearer, we wonder how it'll all end.

In a mushroom cloud reaching for the tropopause,

an airburst of own debris. Will we see ourselves age?

Rubbing the moondust from our eyes,

we keep

walking.